VIOLINJUDY'S

A VIOLIN PIZZA

LEVEL B-C

LEARN TO PLAY VIOLIN

METHOD BOOK WITH SONGS AND ACTIVITIES

FOR BEGINNING VIOLIN STUDENTS

Violin Judy's

VERY FUN VIOLIN COLLECTION

A Violin Pizza by Judy Naillon
Copyright © 2025 ViolinJudy
www.violinjudy.com
ISBN: 978-1-960674-34-0

TABLE OF CONTENTS

NOTE TO TEACHERS/PRACTICE PARENT:

Any Violin Student with minimal experience holding and playing pitches on the A string of a Violin will enjoy and be challenged by this book! For a total beginner *A Violin Twinkle A* or *My First Violin Book* by author Judy "ViolinJudy" Naillon will be more helpful. The pacing of this book is slower than any other supplemental violin books you will find. This allows younger beginners time to really learn to read music as well as play a wide variety of songs. When you establish a firm foundation of technic, listening skills (with free included practice videos) and songs students know and like to play, you'll have a learner who loves music! Playing pieces that are presented in a fun, fresh way engages your learner.

In this book you will find many tools to help your students learn the Violin including info sheets and flashcards.

Pieces in this book are fun to play in group lessons as well! Students who have successfully completed this book can look forward to more skills to learn and fun pieces to master in *Lanes Summer, A Violin Treble, A Violin Fall, A Violin Christmas, A Violin Twinkle Books B and C*, all by author Judy "ViolinJudy" Naillon.

HOW TO USE QR CODES IN THIS BOOK:

SCAN ME

HOW TO SCAN A QR CODE WITH AN IPHONE OR IPAD:

BOTH IPHONES AND IPADS HAVE A QR SCANNER BUILT INTO THE CAMERA.

1. WITH A QR CODE NEARBY, OPEN THE CAMERA ON YOUR IPHONE OR IPAD.

2. POSITION THE CAMERA SO THE QR CODE IS IN FRAME. YOUR IPHONE OR IPAD SHOULD SCAN IT AUTOMATICALLY, WITHOUT ANY INPUT NEEDED FROM YOU. ONCE IT SCANS THE CODE, A NOTIFICATION WILL APPEAR AT THE TOP OF YOUR SCREEN WITH THE LINK TO THE QR CODE`S CONTENT. TAP THIS AND YOU`LL BE BROUGHT TO IT.

HOW TO SCAN A QR CODE WITH AN ANDROID PHONE OR TABLET:

ANDROID DEVICES HAVE THE QR CODE SCANNER BUILT INTO THE CAMERA. HOWEVER, YOU MIGHT NEED TO OPEN A SPECIAL APP TO USE IT.

1. WITH A QR CODE NEARBY, OPEN THE CAMERA ON YOUR ANDROID DEVICE.

2. POSITION THE CAMERA SO THE QR CODE IS IN FRAME. YOUR ANDROID SHOULD SCAN IT AUTOMATICALLY, BUT IF IT DOESN`T, PRESS AND HOLD YOUR FINGER ON IT.

YOU`LL BE GIVEN THE LINK THAT THE QR CODE LEADS TO AND A CHOICE TO OPEN IT, COPY THE URL, OR SHARE IT.

DO'S AND DON'TS FOR VIOLIN:

WASH YOUR HANDS BEFORE YOU PLAY OR PRACTICE VIOLIN.

PLACE YOUR MUSIC ON THE STAND BEFORE YOU OPEN YOUR VIOLIN CASE.

HOLD YOUR BOW WITH THE FROG OR STICK. AVOID TOUCHING THE HAIR. NATURAL OILS ON CLEAN HANDS CAN RUB OFF ON YOUR BOW WHICH PREVENTS ROSIN FROM STICKING TO YOUR BOW.

WHEN TUNING YOUR VIOLIN USE THE FINE TUNERS FOR SMALL PITCH CHANGES. REMEMBER RIGHTY TIGHTY FOR THE PITCH TO GO HIGHER AND LEFTY LOOSEY FOR THE PITCH TO GO LOWER.

DON'T LET YOUR VIOLIN "WIGGLE" BACK AND FORTH WHEN YOU PLAY. YOUR VIOLIN SHOULD STAY STILL AND FLAT AS A TABLETOP. THE VIOLIN IS THE CONSTANT AND THE BOW IS THE VARIABLE.

ROSIN YOUR BOW A LOT WHEN IT'S BRAND NEW. IN THE FUTURE, JUST THREE SWIPES UP AND DOWN BEFORE YOU PRACTICE EACH DAY IS ENOUGH.

DON'T HOLD YOUR BOW LIKE THIS:

USE A MUSIC STAND!
IT WILL HELP YOU HOLD YOUR VIOLIN
FLAT LIKE A TABLE AND YOU'LL
SOUND BETTER!

A VIOLIN PIZZA PREFACE

SET UP YOUR VIOLIN WITH FINGERING TAPES:

Full Size Violin (4/4)
Tape 1 – 35mm (1 3/8 inches)
Tape 2 – 66mm (2 5/8 inches)
Tape 3 – 80mm (3 1/8 inches)
Tape 4 – 106mm (4 1/8 inches)

3/4 Violin
Tape 1 – 32mm (1 1/4 inches)
Tape 2 – 61mm (2 3/8 inches)
Tape 3 – 75 mm (2 7/8 inches)
Tape 4 – 100 mm (3 7/8 inches)

1/2 Violin
Tape 1 – 28mm (1 1/8 inches)
Tape 2 – 54mm (2 1/8 inches)
Tape 3 – 68mm (2 5/8 inches)
Tape 4 – 91mm (3 5/8 inches)

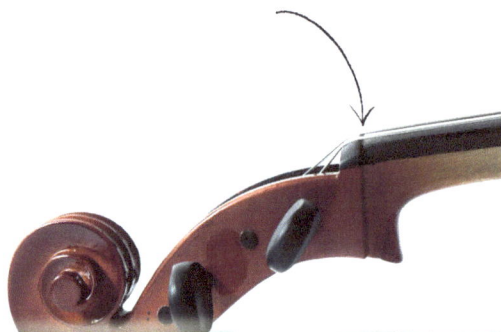

1/4 Violin
Tape 1 – 25mm (1 inch)
Tape 2 – 48mm (1 7/8 inches)
Tape 3 – 60mm (2 3/8 inches)
Tape 4 – 79mm (3 1/8 inches)

You can put a finger tape on your Violin for every finger but you only need two tapes- one for finger #1 in the natural position and one for finger #3. Finger two ALWAYS snuggles up next to finger three in this book. The above chart will help you determine where to place each tape on your specific size violin!
Measure from below the nut -see the above arrow for where to start.

LEARN PARTS OF THE VIOLIN

Sing the Parts of the Violin with your Teacher in a G scale! This is the Scroll, These are the Pegs, This is the Nut...

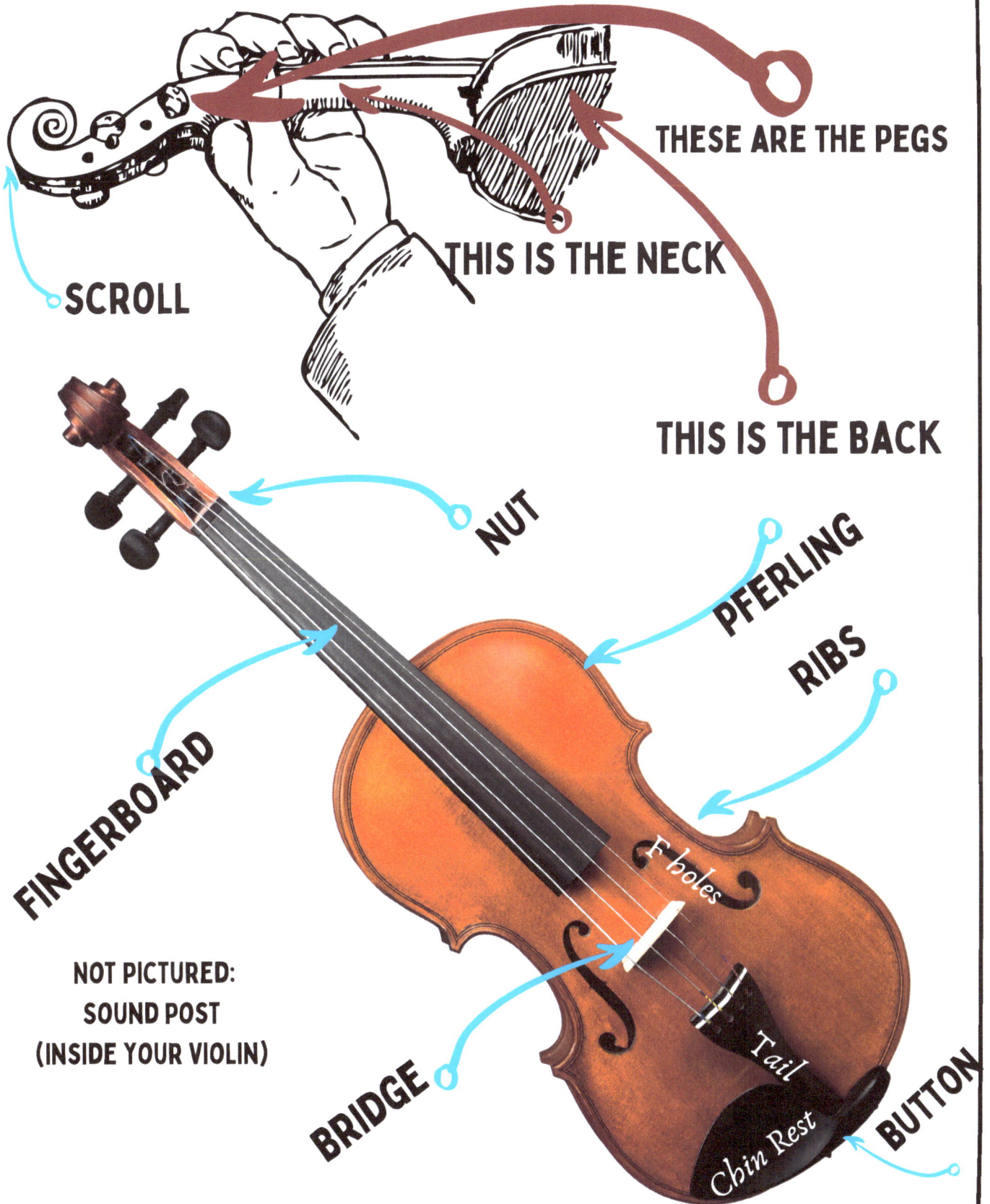

THESE ARE THE PEGS

THIS IS THE NECK

SCROLL

THIS IS THE BACK

NUT

PFERLING

RIBS

FINGERBOARD

F holes

NOT PICTURED:
SOUND POST
(INSIDE YOUR VIOLIN)

BRIDGE

Tail

Chin Rest

BUTTON

PARTS OF THE BOW

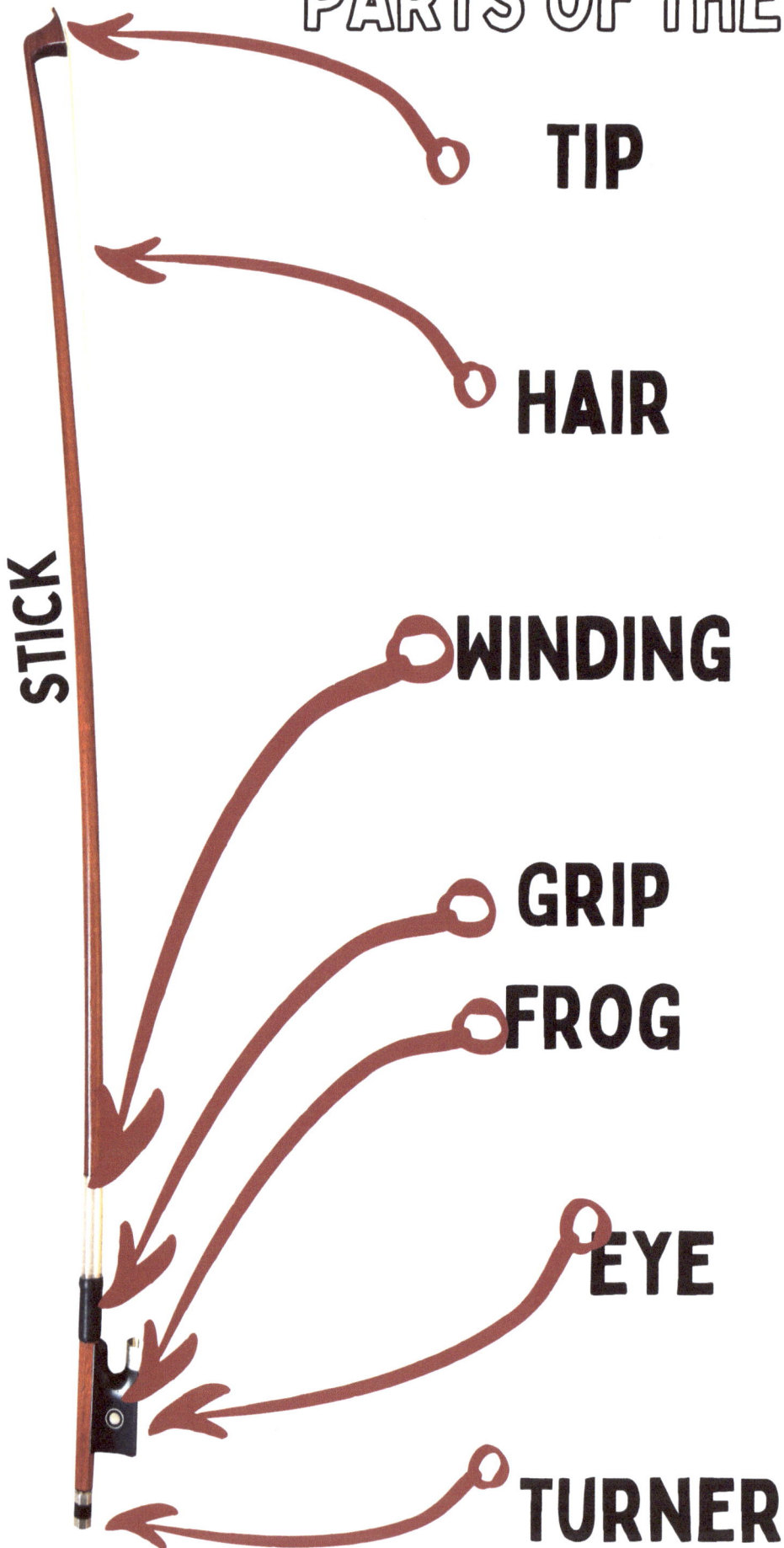

TIP

HAIR

STICK

WINDING

GRIP

FROG

EYE

TURNER

CRAZY PIZZA COMPOSER NAMES

TAKE THE LAST DIGIT OF YOUR AGE

1. MAESTRO
3. LORD/LADY
5. SEÑOR/SEÑORITA
7. HEAD CHEF
9. HEAD CHEESE

2. THE AMAZING
4. MR./MRS.
6. DOCTOR
8. SIR/MADAM
0. CONCERTMASTER

AND THE FIRST LETTER OF YOUR NAME

A. CRUNCHY
B. BASIL
C. SAUCY
D. FEISTY
E. SPICY
F. MEGA
G. MINI
H. PARMESAN
I. PAPRIKA

J. CHEESY
K. BUTTERY
L. GARLICKY
M. SAVORY
N. MUSHROOM
O. PERFECT
P. PERSONAL PAN
Q. MOUTH WATERING
R. PRETZEL

S. CHEWY
T. CRISPY
U. SALTY
V. CLASSY
W. ZESTY
X. STUFFED CRUST
Y. OLIVE
Z. SIZZLING

AND YOUR BIRTH MONTH

JANUARY-STUFFED CRUST PIZZA
FEBRUARY-PIZZA PARTY
MARCH-PEPPERONI PIZZA
APRIL-SUPREME PIZZA
MAY-HAWAIIAN PIZZA
JUNE-DESSERT PIZZA

JULY-TACO PIZZA
AUGUST-CHEESE PIZZA
SEPTEMBER-BREADSTICKS
OCTOBER-SINGLE SLICE
NOVEMBER-DOUBLE SLICE
DECEMBER-PARTY PIZZA

TREBLE CLEF-NOTES YOU NEED TO KNOW

On line 2 write the letter in the note head and the finger above or below.

Then play each note-remember these are whole notes and get 4 counts each.

TREBLE CLEF-NOTES YOU NEED TO KNOW

On line 2 write the letter in the note head and the finger above or below.

Then play each note-remember these are whole notes and get 4 counts each.

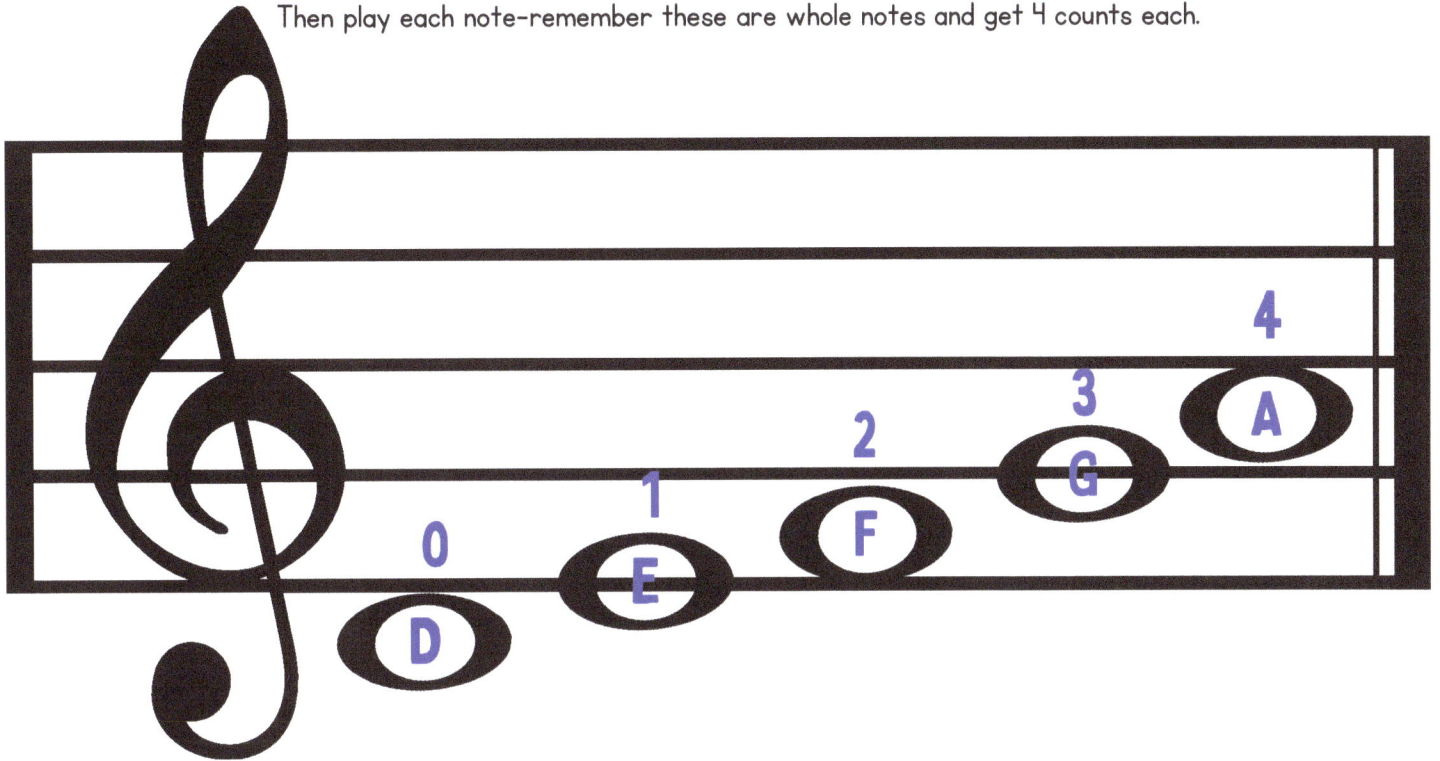

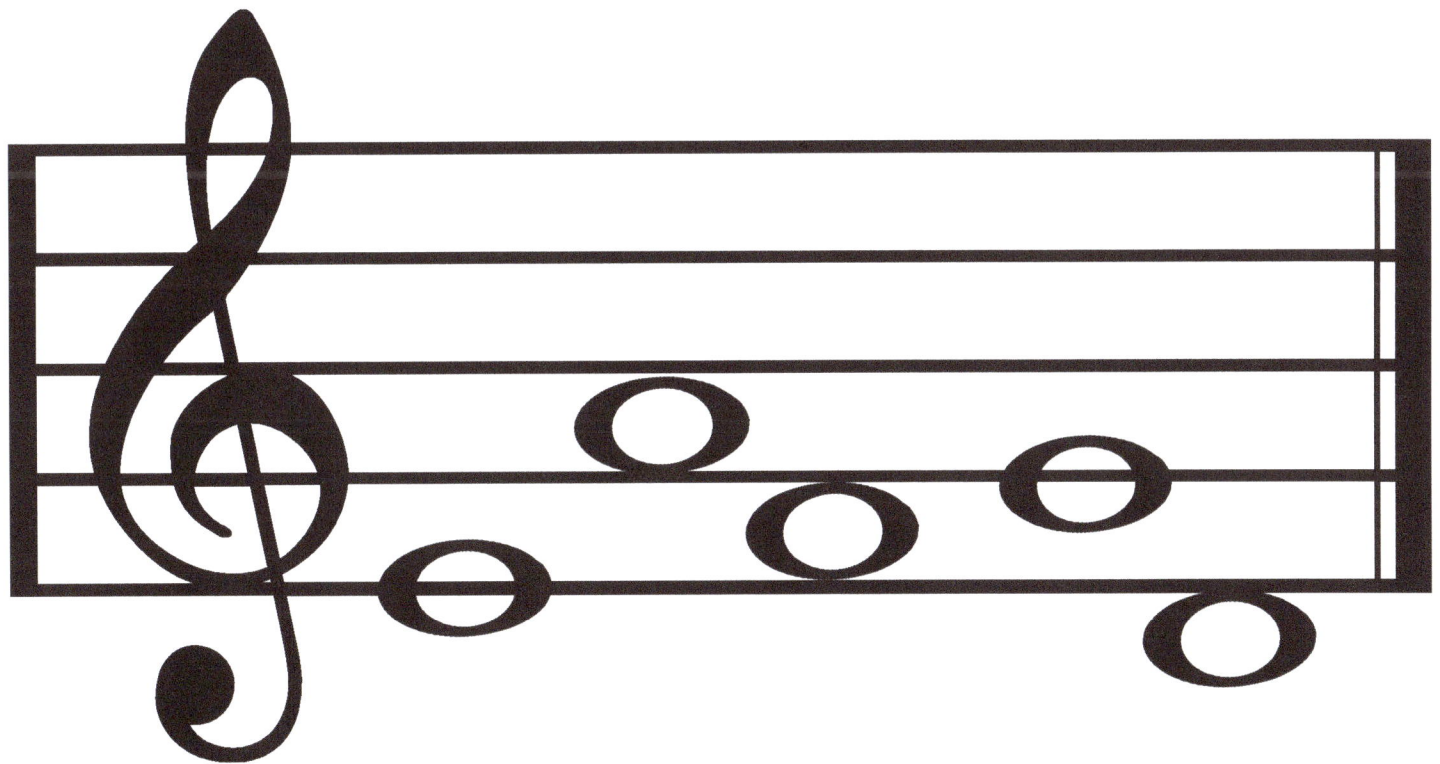

TREBLE CLEF-NOTES YOU NEED TO KNOW

Take a careful look at these notes on the E string!

0 — E
LOW 1 — F
NORMAL 1 — F SHARP
LOW 2 — G

THE WHITE TAPES ON THIS VIOLIN SHOW WHERE FINGERS 1 & 3 NORMALLY LIVE. ON E STRING LOW ONE IS NEAR THE NUT/SCROLL (PURPLE ARROW.) LOW 2 IS NEAR FINGER 1 (ORANGE ARROW.) HIGH 2 IS WHERE FINGER 2 IS PLACED CLOSE TO FINGER 3. NEED MORE HELP? SCAN THE QR CODE FOR A VIDEO DEMONSTRATION!

Take a careful look at these notes on the A & D string!

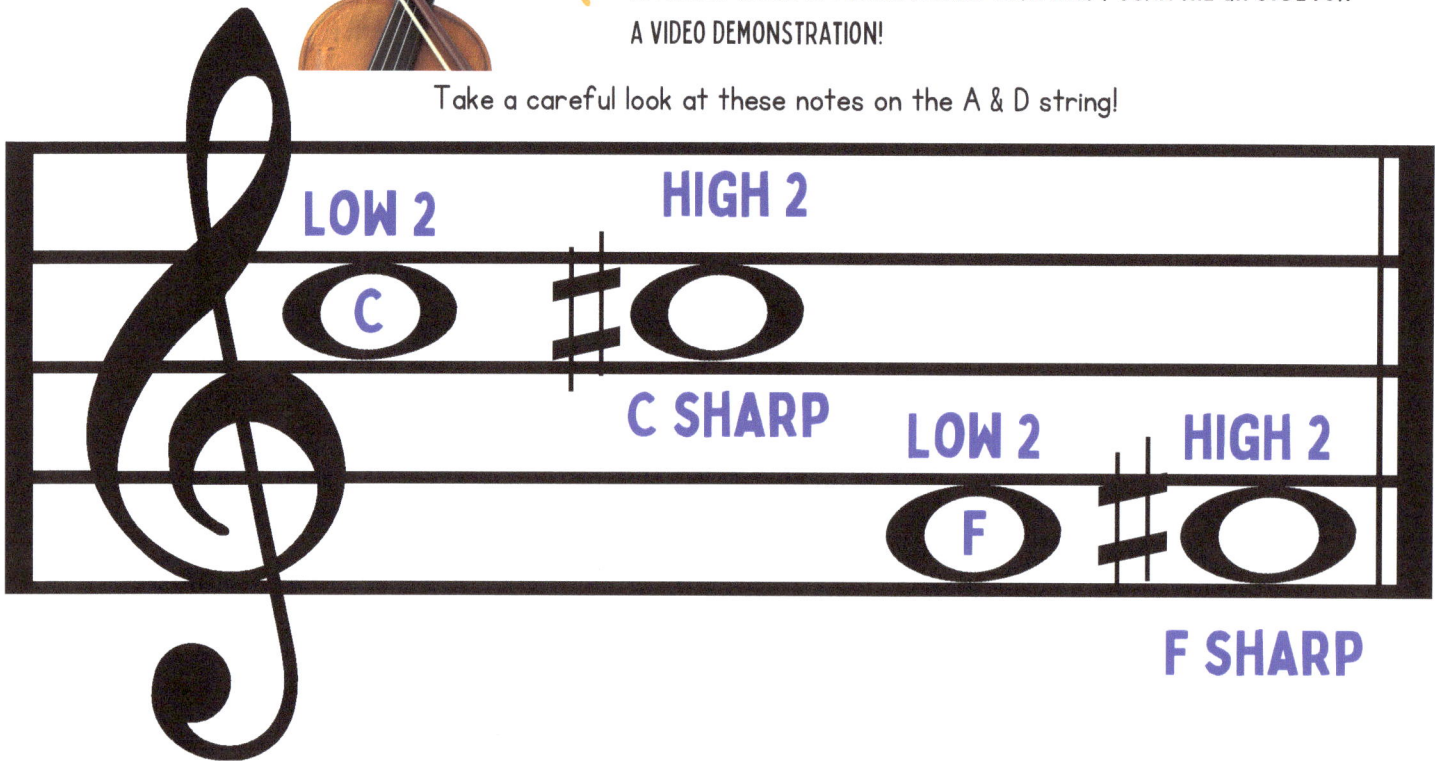

LOW 2 — C
HIGH 2 — C SHARP

LOW 2 — F
HIGH 2 — F SHARP

PIZZA PIZZA

JUDY NAILLON

Piz - za   Pi -za   it's   a   treat!

Piz - za   Pi -za   fun   to   eat!

Crunchy   crust goes   in my   tum -   my

Goo -ey   cheese is   yum   my!

14 MY FAVORITE PIZZA

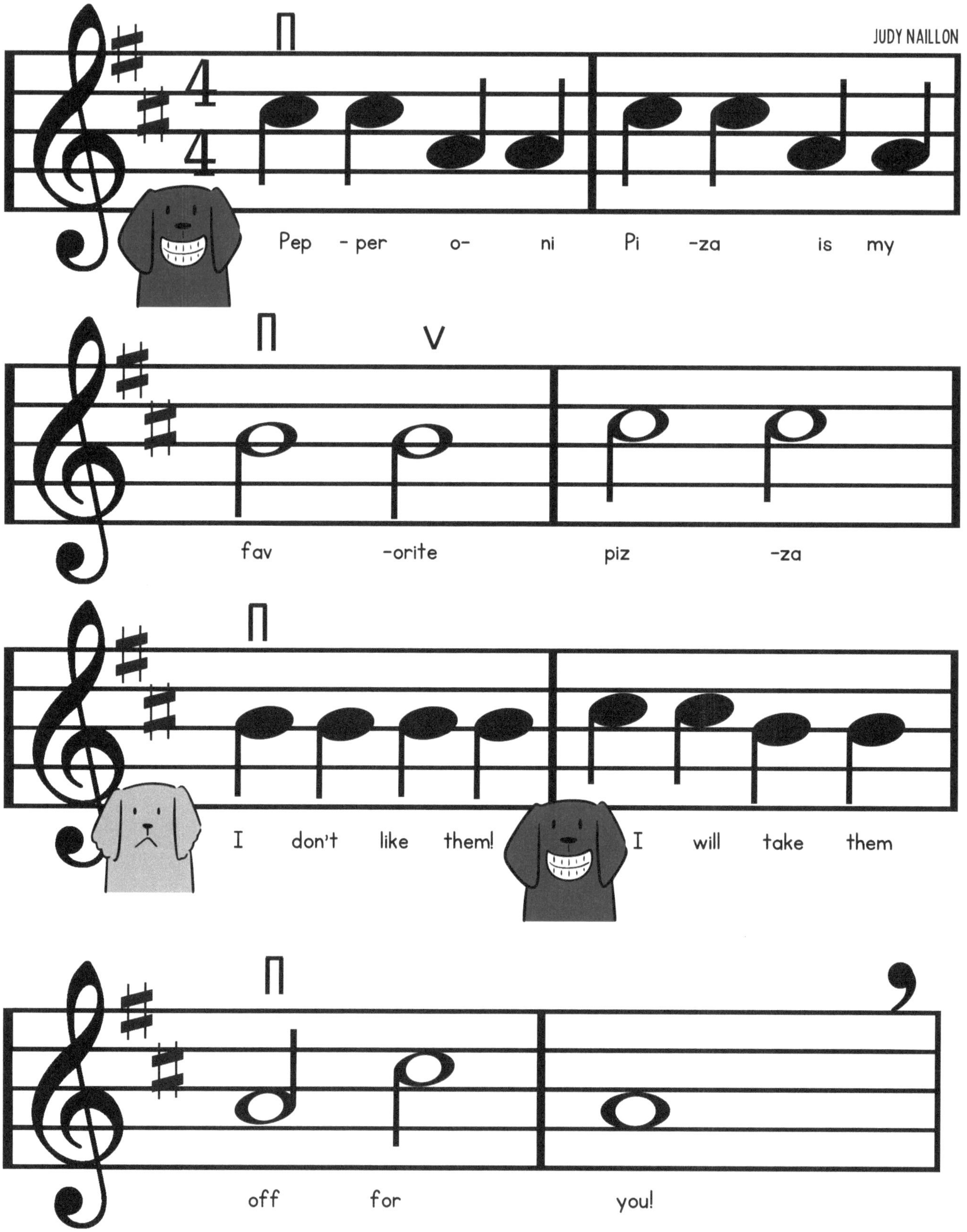

JUDY NAILLON

Pep - per o- ni Pi -za is my

fav -orite piz -za

I don't like them! I will take them

off for you!

Cheese   piz – za,   Cheese   is   my

fav–   orite   piz   –za

Let's   get   half   and   half   and   split   a

pie   for   two!

16

PIZZA CAT

JUDY NAILLON

I like piz – za hot,

I like piz – za cold,

I like piz – za in the box

five days old!

A VIOLIN PIZZA P.9

PIZZA CAT

You like piz – za hot,

But not piz – za old,

I like piz – za in the trash

nine days old! (Yuck!)

18 TARANTELLA NAPOLETANA

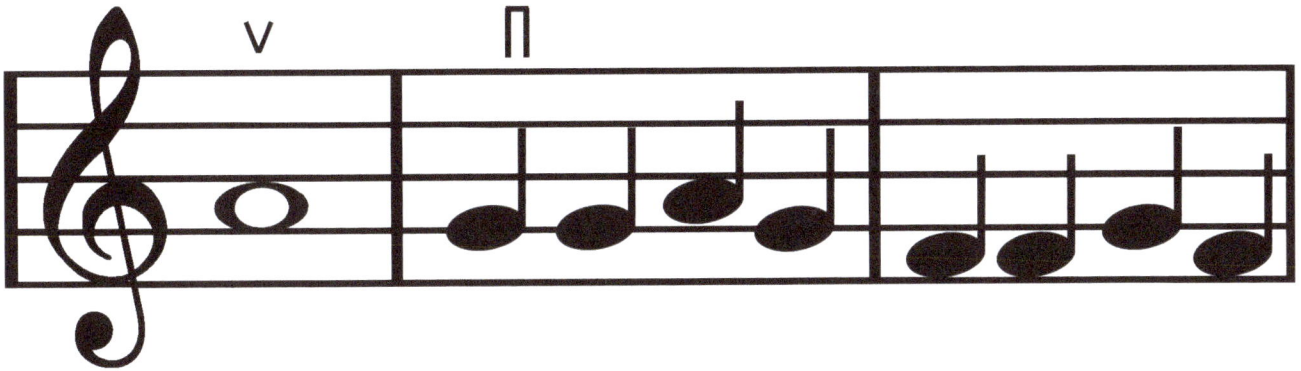

TRY PLAYING THESE "LOW" FINGERS:

THIS VIOLIN HAS WHITE TAPES WHERE FINGER 1 AND 3
NORMALLY GO. WHEN YOU SEE A FLAT IN FRONT OF B
YOU PLACE YOUR FINGER LOWER BACK BY THE NUT OF
THE VIOLIN (PURPLE ARROW.)

EVEN THOUGH ONLY THE FIRST NOTE HAS A FLAT
SYMBOL BEFORE IT, ALL THE REMAINING NOTES
OF THE SAME PITCH ARE FLAT IN THE MEASURE!

THESE ARE STILL B FLATS!

THESE ARE STILL F NATURALS-LOW 2 ON D!

WHEN YOU DO NOT SEE A SHARP SIGN AT THE BEGINNING OF THE LINE (KEY SIGNATURE) OR RIGHT BEFORE
THE NOTE THEN 2 ON D (F NATURAL) IS "LOW" OR SNUGGLED UP NEXT TO FINGER 1 (ORANGE ARROW)

20

O SOLE MIO

COMPOSER: DI CAPUA
ARRANGED BY: MRS. JUDY NAILLON

O SOLE MIO

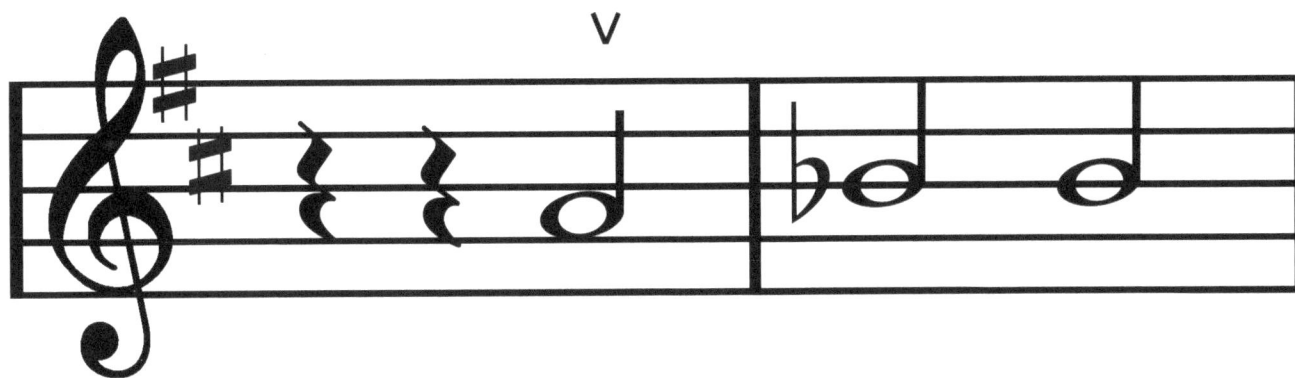

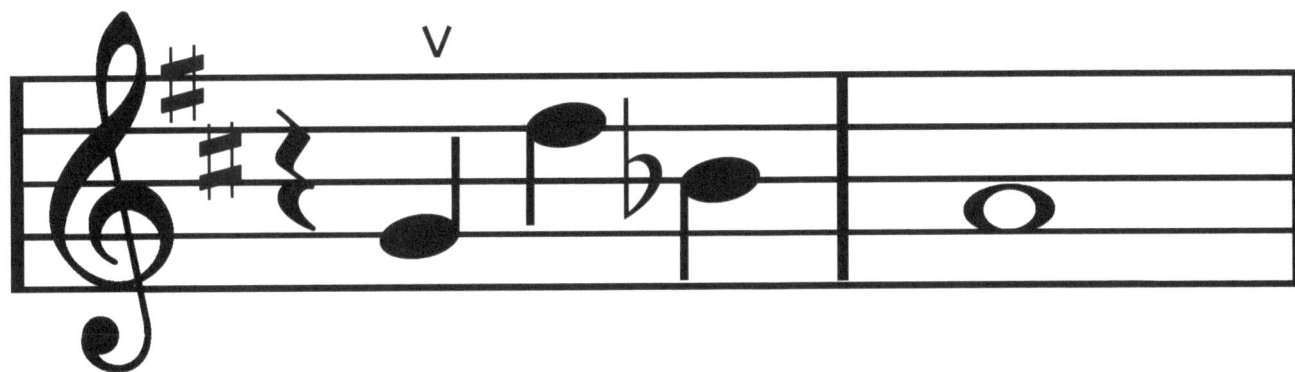

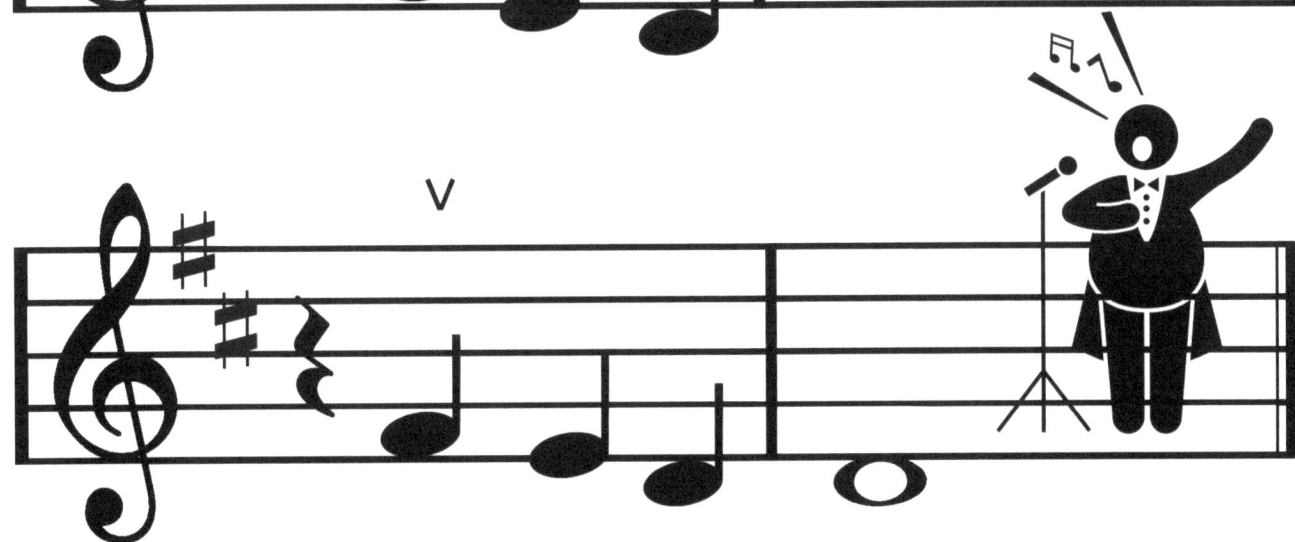

BELLA CIAO

THIS FOLK SONG WAS ORIGINALLY SUNG BY ITALIAN WOMEN WHILE WORKING IN THE RICE FIELDS.
THESE WORKERS WERE CALLED MONDINAS!

FOLK SONG
ARRANGED BY: MRS. JUDY NAILLON

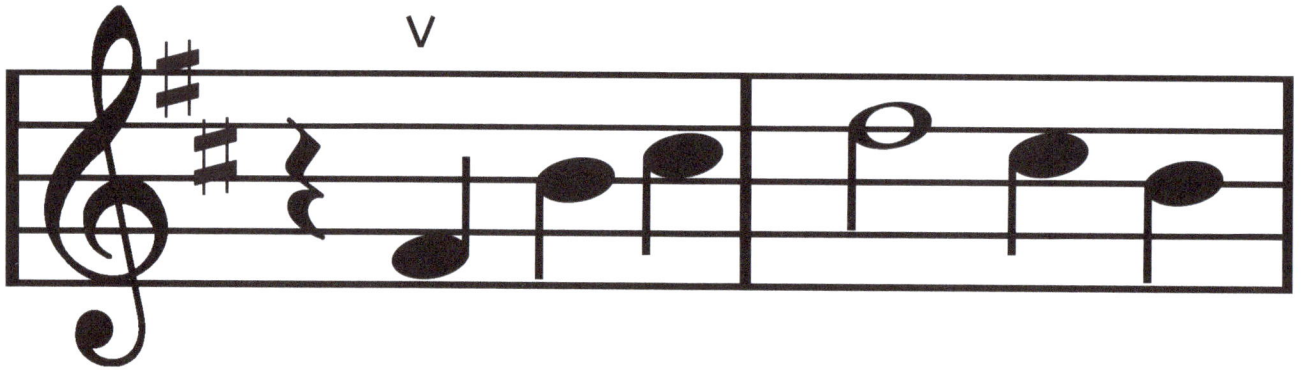

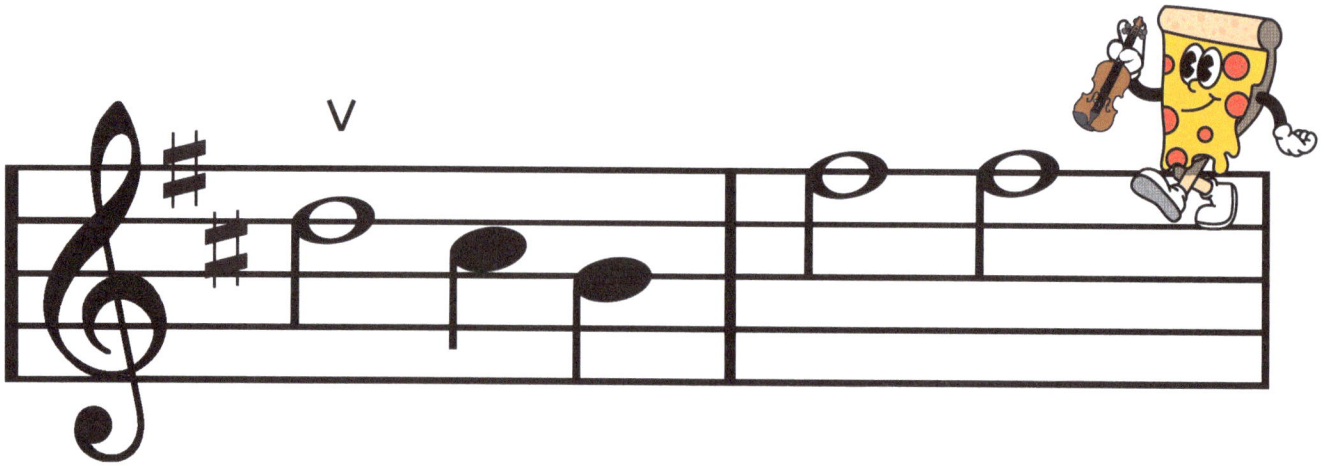

BELLA CIAO

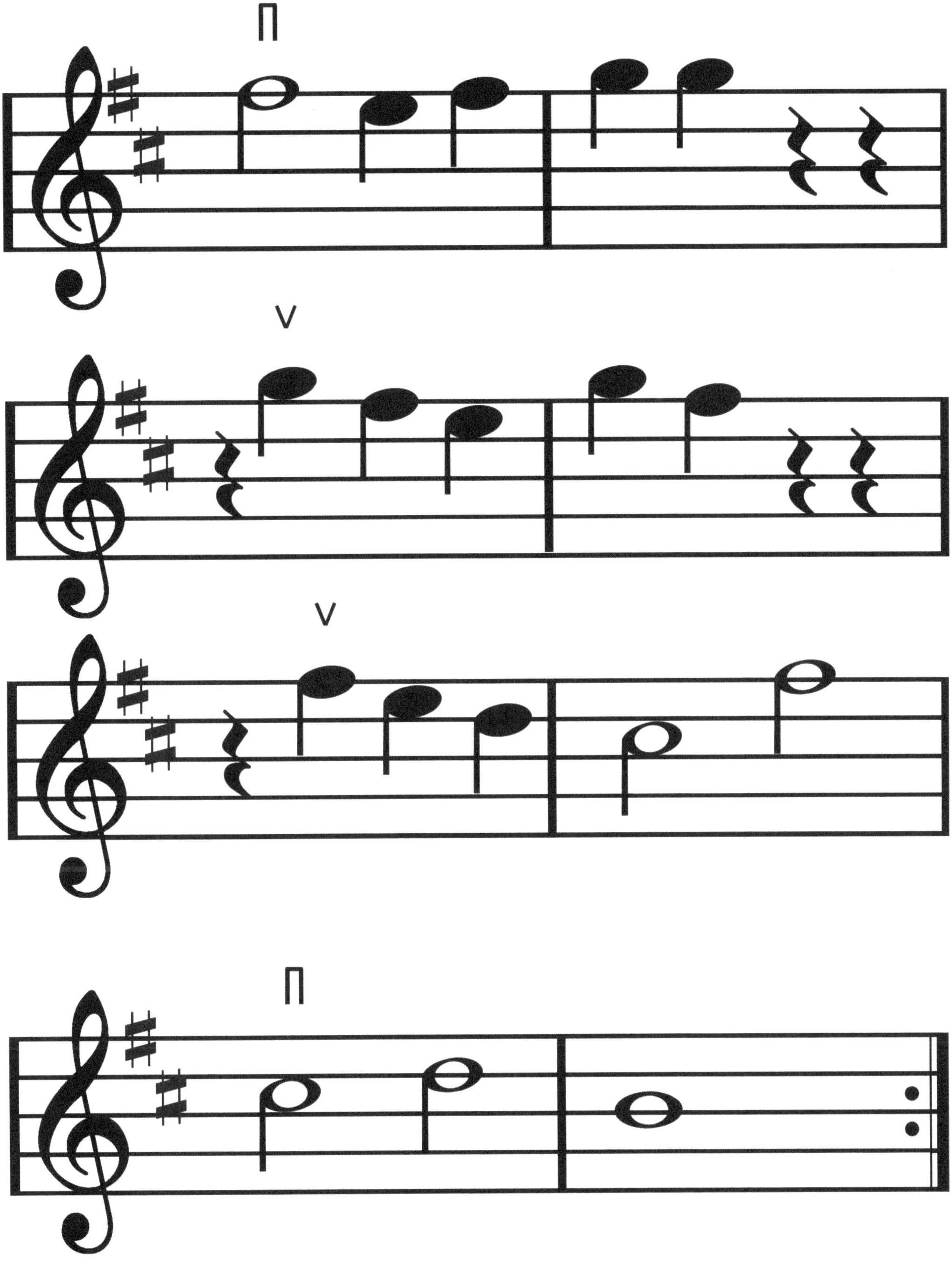

24 FUNICULI FUNICULA

MANY PEOPLE THINK THIS IS AN OLD ITALIAN FOLK SONG HOWEVER IT WAS WRITTEN BY FRIENDS
TO CELEBRATE THE GRAND OPENING OF A FUNICULAR CABLE CAR!

LUIGI DENZA
ARRANGED BY: JUDY NAILLON

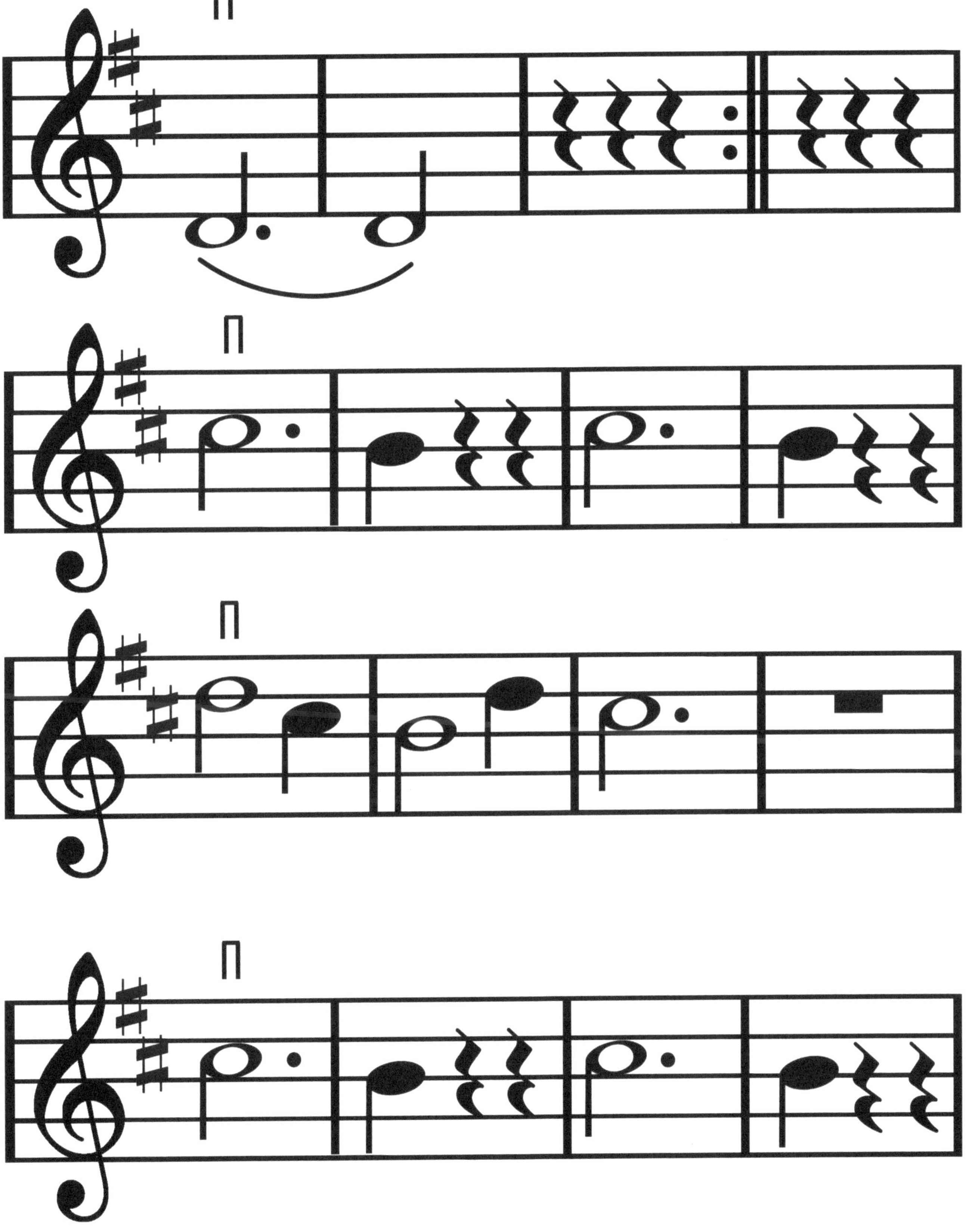

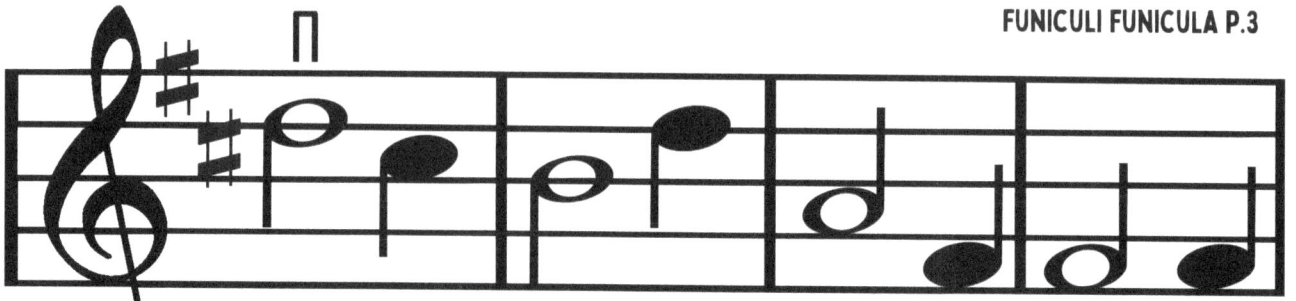

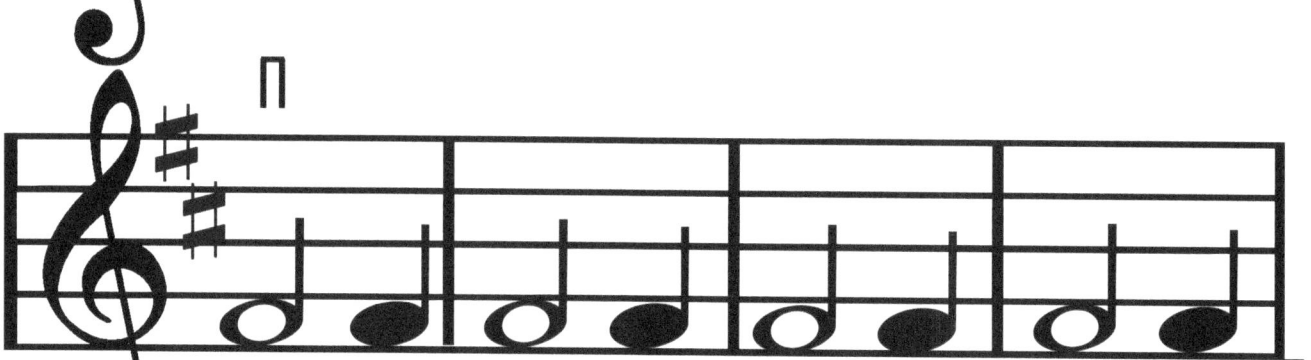

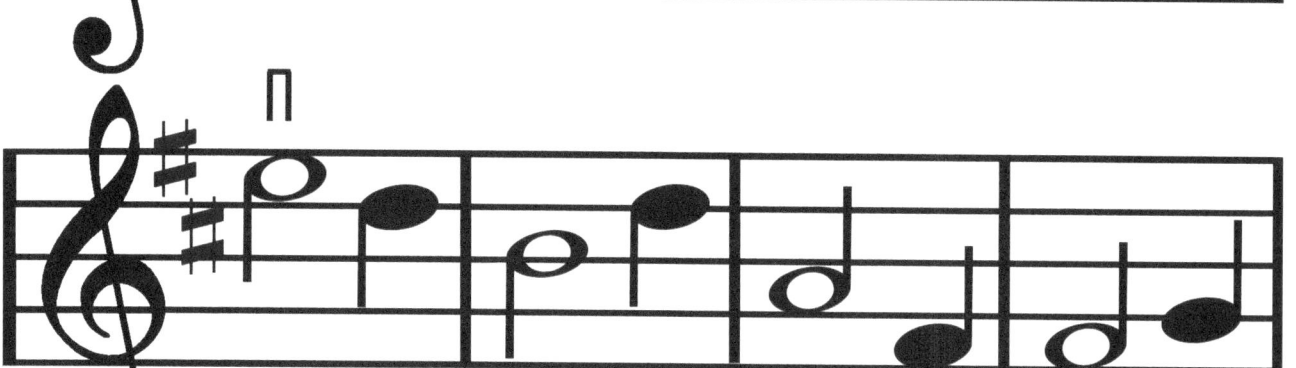

26 O MIO BABBINO CARO

PUCCINI
ARRANGED BY: JUDY NAILLON

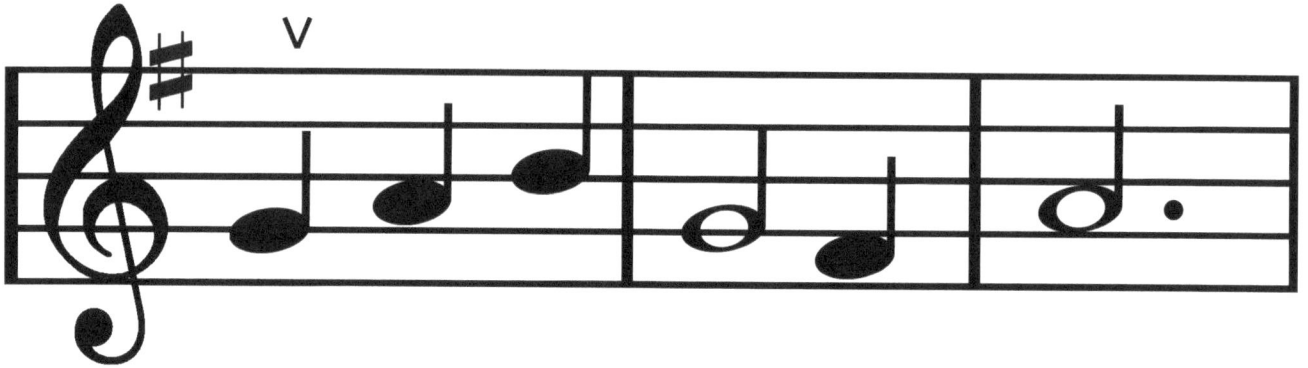

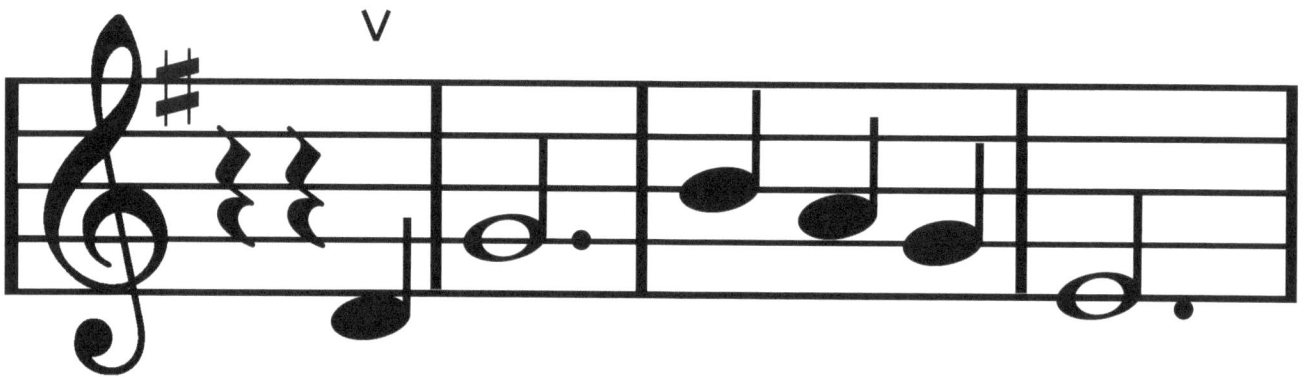

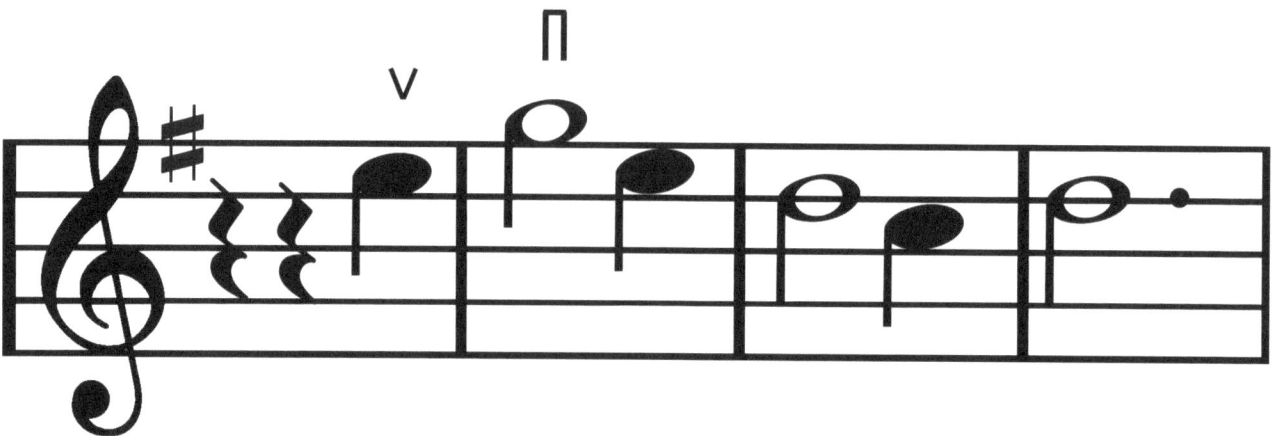

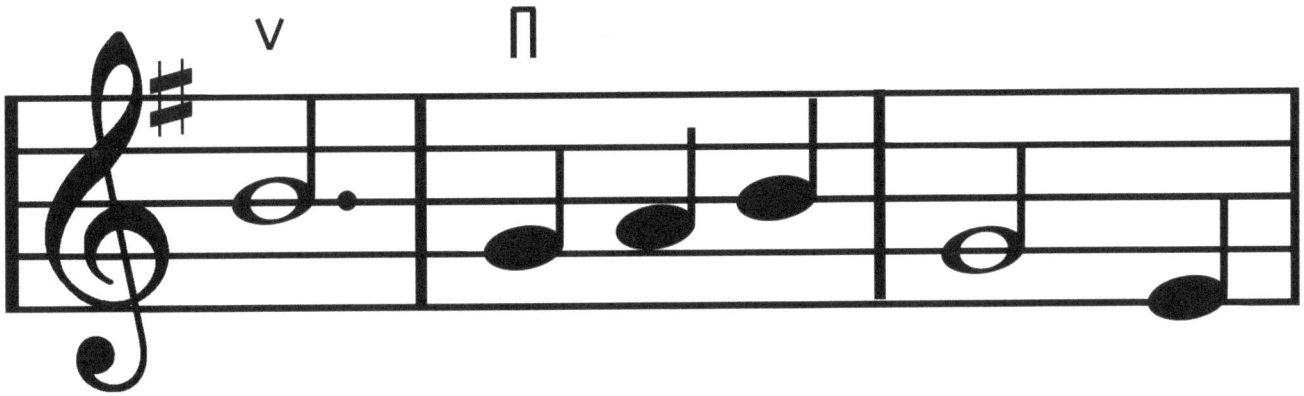

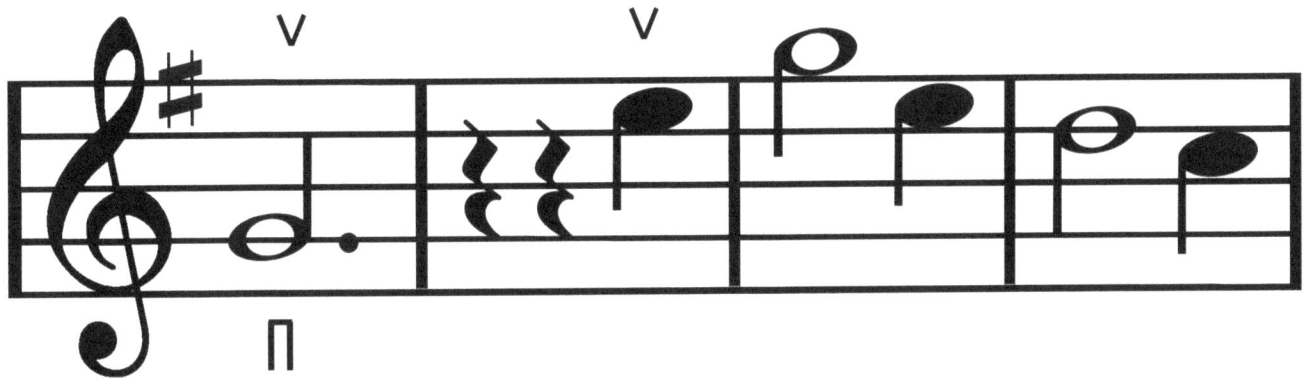

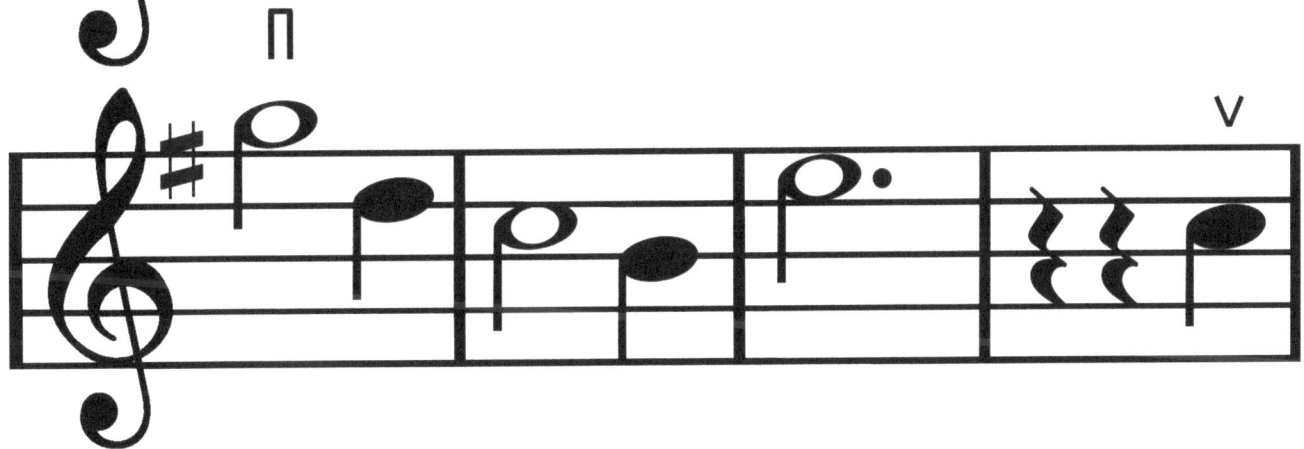

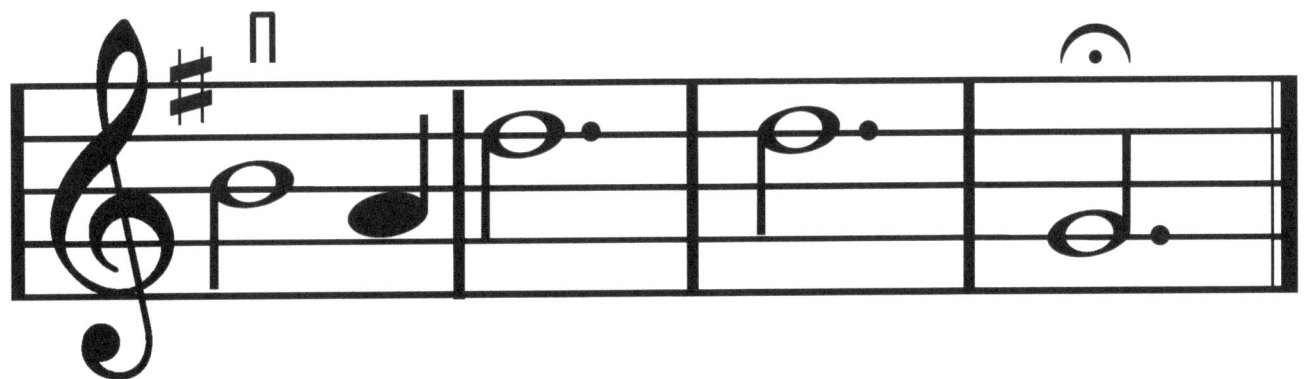

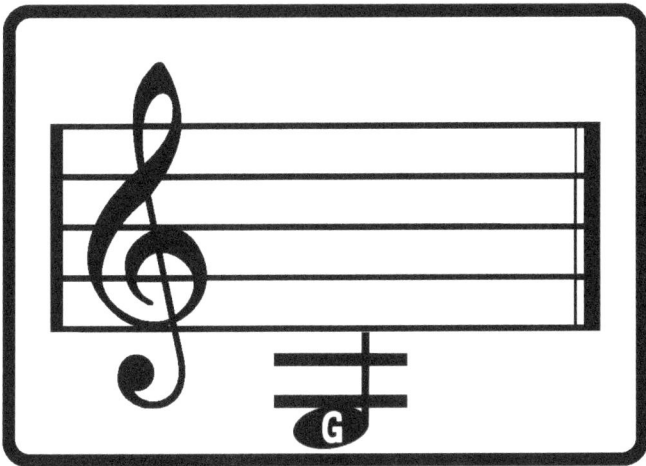

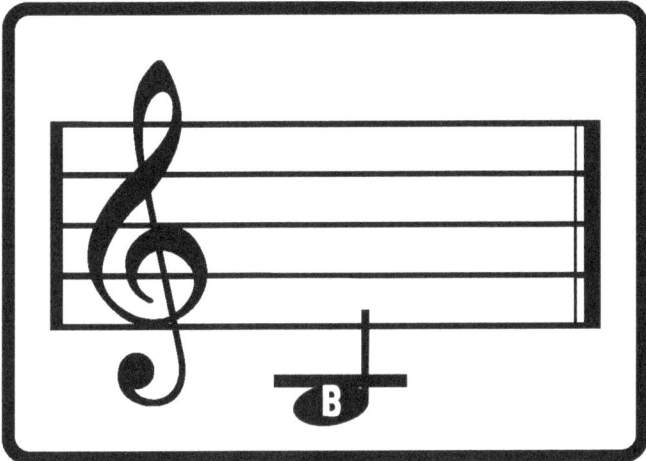

1 ON G STRING

OPEN G STRING

3 ON G STRING

2 ON G STRING

1 ON D STRING

OPEN D STRING

3 ON D STRING

2 ON D STRING

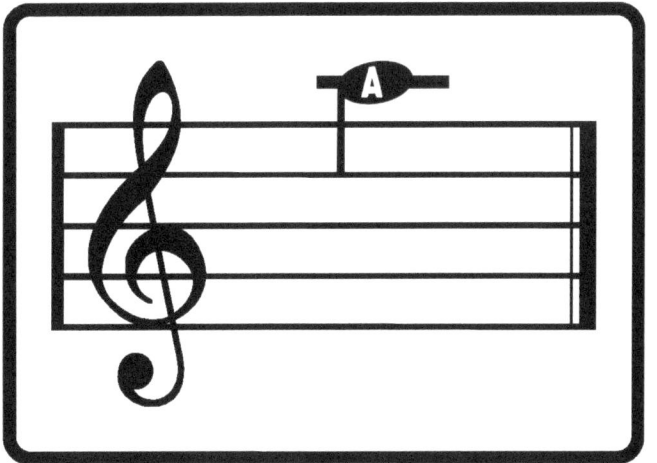

1 ON A STRING

OPEN A STRING

3 ON A STRING

2 ON A STRING

1 ON E STRING

OPEN E STRING

3 ON E STRING

2 ON E STRING

Violin Judy

Mrs. Judy Naillon, B.M. Violin Performance or "ViolinJudy" is a dedicated and enthusiastic independent piano and violin teacher, composer, and professional violinist. Her work consists of her large private music studio, as well as playing with her string quartet and Wichita Symphony Orchestra. She served as a church musician for over 20 years and is active in leadership in the musicians' union. She loves coming up with creative ideas to help both students and teachers be successful and blogs about it all at www.ViolinJudy.com and for Alfred's Music Publishers. When she is not writing new Violin books she loves spending time with her family and little dog Pom.

BOOK LEVEL CHART FOR THE **VERY FUN VIOLIN LIBRARY**

VIOLIN GRADE	FUN VIOLIN LEVEL	MAIN CONCEPTS
PRE-TWINKLE	**A**	RHYTHMS, FINGERS 1,2,3 ON A FINGER 1 ON E
LEVEL 1A	**B**	NOTE READING 1,2,3 ON A OPEN D & 1 ON E
LEVEL IB	**C**	NOTE READING ON D, A & E STRINGS, FINGER 4
LEVEL 2A	**D**	NOTE READING ON ALL STRINGS
LEVEL 2B	**E**	INTRO TO 3RD POSITION & VIBRATO

CERTIFICATE
OF ACHIEVEMENT

This awarded to :

_ _ _ _ _ _ _ _ _ _ _ _ _ _ _ _ _ _

for the achievement of the completion of:

_ _ _ _ _ _ _ _ _ _ _ _ _ _ _ _ _ _

Teacher   Date

www.ingramcontent.com/pod-product-compliance
Lightning Source LLC
LaVergne TN
LVHW072057070426
835508LV00002B/133